J. H. Tenney, E. A. Hoffman

Temperance Jewels

J. H. Tenney, E. A. Hoffman

Temperance Jewels

ISBN/EAN: 9783337135751

Printed in Europe, USA, Canada, Australia, Japan

Cover: Foto ©Thomas Meinert / pixelio.de

More available books at **www.hansebooks.com**

TEMPERANCE JEWELS.

Sound Ye the Trumpet!

Mrs. E. C. Ellsworth.

J. H. Tenney.

1. O sound ye the trum - pet! The foe is at
2. O sound ye the trum - pet! And march to the
3. Drive back - ward the temp - ter! Je - ho - vah will

hand; With vice there's a con - flict; There's war in the land.
fray; Be brave and be val - iant, We'll soon win the day.
send His an - gels to help you, His cause to de - fend.

CHORUS.

Then sound ye the trumpet With notes loud and clear! O call to the

1.
ser- vice, Till all vol - un - teer!

2.
ser - vice, Till all vol - un - teer!

4

I will Win or Die.

E. A. HOFFMAN.   J. A. TENNEY.

1. I stand on the field of bat - tle, Pledged to win or
2. Firm - ly stand with faith and cour - age, Pledged to win or
3. I will stand be - side my Cap - tain, Pledged to win or

die; Fear- less earn - est in the fight, Bear- ing sword and ar - mor
die; Foes a - wait us ev - ery- where, Foes that we must brave- ly
die; Faith- ful - ly my sword I'll wield, Till the van - ished foe- man

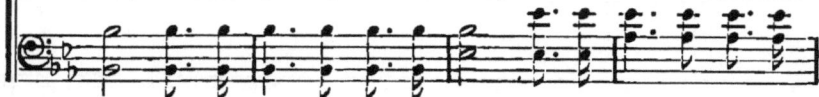

bright, Bravely struggling for the right, I will win or die!
dare Till the vic - to - ry we share, Till we win or die!
yield Till we drive them from the field, Till we win or die!

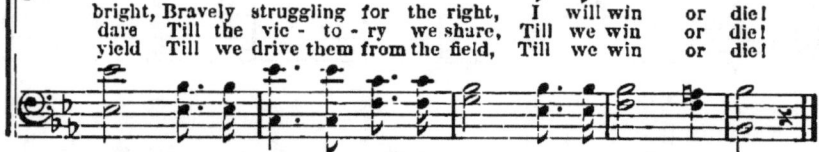

CHORUS.

Yes, I'll win or die; I will win or die; In the

strug - gle for the vic - to - ry I will win or die!

Stand, Firmly Stand!

E. A. HOFFMAN.

J. H. TENNEY.

1. Stand, firm - ly stand! A no - ble, val - iant band; For temp'rance and
2. Stand, firm - ly stand! U - nit - ed, heart and hand; Press no - bly, bold-
3. Stand, firm - ly stand! Defend our bless - ed land From ev - 'ry sub-

the right, Your for - ces all u - nite, And cast in - to the strife The
- ly on, Till vic - to - ry is won, Till notes of tri - umph thrill O'er
- tle foe, From ev - 'ry tide of woe; Stand brave- ly in your might; Stand

CHORUS.

strength of all your life. Stand, firm-ly stand! Stand, firm-ly stand!
ev - 'ry vale and hill.
bravely for the right.

Stand, firm - ly stand for the right! On, bravely on!
firmly stand for the right,

On, bravely on! On, bravely on! bravely on in your might!

By permission.

6 **Proudly Raise the Glorious Banner.**

MRS. E. W. CHAPMAN.   J. H. TENNEY.

Allegro.

1. In the strength of God we'll ral - ly, Round our glo - rious flag will
2. We will scat - ter beams of kind-ness, Lead the stray-ing souls to
3. Rous - ing some from death-like slumber, For-ward we will march a -

stand; Or will march thro' plain and valley For the res - cue of our land.
light, Guide the lost, who grope in blindness, To the path of truth and right.
long, Till, with trophies with-out num-ber, We will sing the tri - umph song.

CHORUS.

Proudly raise . . . the glo - rious ban - ner; Float it
Proud-ly raise

high . . . up - on the air; Shout a - loud . . .
Float it high   Shout a - loud

a glad ho - san - na; Praise to Him who an - swers prayer.

Copyright, 1879, by OLIVER DITSON & Co.

The Battalions are Marching. 7

E. A. H.   REV. ELISHA A. HOFFMAN.

1. The tread of migh-ty arm-ies rolls O'er mountain, plain, and
2. The air is bright-en-ing a-round, The skies are grow-ing
3. A cho-rus grand and full and deep, Rolls up-ward to the
4. March on-ward to the bat-tle-field; The Lord thy strength will

sea:
clear;
sky;
be;

The hosts of God are mar-shall-ing For
The heav'n of heav'ns is coming down, Re-
A tri-umph song of praise to God Who
Go for-ward in the Master's name, As-

The hosts of God are marshalling,
The heav'n of heav'ns is com-ing down,
A triumph song of praise to God,
Go forward in the Master's name,

are marshall-ing
is coming down,
of praise to God,
the Master's name,

CHORUS.

glo-rious vic-to-ry!
demption's dawn is near.
gives the vic-to-ry.
sured of vic-to-ry.

O form your bat-tal-ions and

march! march! march! on! march! on! O
march on! march on! march on! march on! march

form your bat-tal-ions and march on, On to vic-to-ry!
march on! march on!

Look for the Lights.

MRS. E. C. ELLSWORTH. J. H. TENNEY.

1. Look for the lights, my broth-er;.... What do the sig - nals tell?
2. Is it the down-train, brother?.... What is the grade be - low?
3. Put on the brakes, my broth-er;.... Stop in thy mad ca - reer;

How doth thy journey prosper? Say, shall the end be well? Hast thou the right track
Say, is the speed increasing? What do the way-marks show? Onward thy life is
Know of the route before thee; See if the track be clear; Just a mis-take, my

tak - en? Is it the one for thee? Will it ensure thy passage
hasting, Bearing thee swift-ly by; Art thou in safe - ty passing?
broth-er, Just to be wrong to - day, How shall it be to - mor-row,

CHORUS.

True to thy des - ti - ny? Look for the lights, my broth - er;....
Is there no dan - ger nigh?
When thou art far a - way?

rit.

What do the signals tell? How doth thy journey prosper? Say, shall the end be well.

Go to Jesus.

1. Is the con-flict strong with-in thee, And thy weak re-sist-ance small?
2. Do thy out-ward foes as-sail thee, Meet-ing thee with taunts and scorn?
3. Has thy life been dark and sin-ful? Is thy heart now far from God?

Go to Je-sus; he will help thee By his grace to conquer all.
Go to Je-sus; he will hear thee; Once he wore the crown of thorn.
Go to Je-sus; he will wash thee In his own most precious blood.

CHORUS.

Go to Je-sus, go to Je-sus; Go and tell him, tell him all thy care; Go to all thy care;

Je-sus, go to Je-sus; Go, and he will hear thy prayer. will hear thy prayer.

Copyright, 1879, by Oliver Ditson & Co.

Hark! for Gentle Voices.

MRS. E. C. ELLSWORTH.   Arranged from BLOCKLEY by J. H. T.

DUET.

1. Hark! for gen - tle   voi - ces   Whis - per to thee with -
2. Look! thy friends are weep - ing,   Weep - ing thy fate to
3. Hark! the Spir - it   whis - pers   Urg - ing no more de -

in,   Quick thy soul to   res - cue
see;   Hearts, with sor - row ach - ing,
lay;   Christ his aid has prom - ised,

From the dark curse of sin;   O shall the wine - cup,
Earn - est - ly pray for thee;   Wilt thou the glass be
Prom - ised his help to - day;   O wilt thou drown these

charm - ing, Still lead thy feet a - stray? Nay;
drain - ing, That hides the ad - der's sting, The
voi - ces With - in the poi - soned bowl, And

though the wine be spark - ling, Renounce that cup to - day. Then
cup that pain and sor - row And woe a - lone can bring?
drink the cup that spark - les With ru - in for thy soul?

CHORUS.

Hark! for gen - tle voi - ces Whis - per to thee with - in,

Now thy soul to res - cue From the dark curse of sin.

Flash the Toplights.

ARTHUR W. FRENCH.   FRANK M. DAVIS.

1. Out to sea, 'mid storm-y gales, As the good ship Temp'rance
2. As the night and shad-ows creep O - ver all the might - y
3. Stead - y stand be - side the helm, Tho' the wa - ter 'most o'er-
4. Rocks and reefs and shift-ing bars, With, per-haps, no guid - ing

sails, Let each warn-ing sig - nal light Up a - loft be burning br'ght.
deep, Safe - ly set a - right in care Ev - ery warn- ing sig - nal there.
whelm, Soon up-right- ed you shall be; Let the lamps shine out to sea.
stars, Dan-ger lies on ev - 'ry hand; Trumpet forth this one command.

CHORUS.

Flash the top - lights far and wide! Tem - pest tossed up - on the

tide; Some poor wreck'd one they may save As they gleam a- cross the wave.

From "CRYSTAL NOTES," by permission.

Spike the Guns.

ARTHUR W. FRENCH.　　　　　　　　　W. IRVING HARTSHORN.

With vigor.

1. Forward, sol-diers! storm the ramparts; Form your ranks a - gain;
2. Hand to hand is now the con - flict; Stead - y as you go;
3. Fear not ye the din of bat - tle; Up the breast-works throng;
4. Proud-ly hold what by your val - or You have no - bly won:

Beat - en back, be not dis - couraged; Up, and on a - gain!
Mark the ty - rants, let your sa - bre Crush at ev - 'ry blow.
Yield no van - tage, till, tri - umphant, Yours the vic - tor's song.
More than conquerors in the con-flict Ev - 'ry temp'rance son.

CHORUS.

Spike the guns, and o'er the ram-parts! In the bat - tle's glare

Let the glo - rious temp'rance standard Wave tri - umphant there.

My Boy is Out To-Night.

MRS. E. C. ELLSWORTH.   J. H. TENNEY.

1. My boy is out to-night, Once bright and fair! Temp-
2. My boy is out to-night, Far, far a - way! The
3. My boy is out to-night, Mine eyes are dim With
4. My boy is out to-night, Go, search, and see; And

ta - tion, fierce and wild, Has swept a - way my child I know not where!
tempter saw him pass, And with one fa - tal glass Led him a - stray.
weeping and with tears, And watching in my fears, For him, for him.
if you find my boy, O bring him back with joy To God and me!

CHORUS.

My boy is out to - night! My boy! my boy! Oh!

I for him could die, If that would bring him nigh, My poor, lost boy!

By permission of J. H. TENNEY.

Hold the Light.

15

J. H. TENNEY.

1. Many a soul on life's dark o-cean, With no helm or oar,
2. Broth - er Chris -tian, thine the la - bor, By the light of love,
3. Like the light- house watcher keep-ing Ev - 'ry bea - con bright,
4. Bor - row torch - es from the al - tar, Blaz - ing like the sun;

Bat - tling with the waves' commo-tion, Seeks a qui - et shore.
To as - sist thy err - ing broth -er To the port a - bove.
Wak - ing while the world is sleep-ing, Wrapt in thick - est night.
Hold them up, nor flag, nor fal - ter Till thy work is done.

CHORUS.

Hold the light for souls in dark - ness; Hold the light up high;

Hold the light still high - er, broth - er, Or those souls will die!

Copyright, 1879, by OLIVER DITSON & Co.

16 # The World is Moving On.

Words and Music by R. LOWRY.

1. A song, a song to-day, For those who meet the fray, Where
2. The truth in du-rance long, Is com-ing forth with song; The
3. Then shout and ring a-gain The new e-van-gel strain That

sunshine struggles with the night; The cloud of er-ror's reign Is
na-tions catch the swell-ing cry; Op-press-sion, crime, and greed, And
ush-ers in the ris-ing day; The com-ing a-ges wait At

lift-ing from the plain, And brave hearts bat-tle for the right.
su-per-sti-tion's creed Are stricken, driv-en out to die.
Freedom's gold-en gate, And brave hearts throng a-bout the way.

By permission.

CHORUS.

Oh, the world is mov- ing on! The world is mov- ing on; From

low - land and from val - ley, On mountain- tops they ral - ly; The

bat - tle bow is strung; The ban - ner is out - flung: And a

gi - ant wrong no more is strong, For the world is mov - ing on!

Upward or Downward?

ARTHUR W. FRENCH. W. O. PERKINS.

(May be sung in unison, the organ playing the harmony.)

1 Up - ward or downward, which shall it be? Stop for a mo -ment, con-
2. Up - ward or downward, which shall it be? This is the ques-tion of
3. Up - ward or downward, make up your mind; 'Twill be too late by and

- sid - er and see; Pon - der it o - ver; think which is best;
ques- tions to thee; One or the oth - er; fail - ure, suc- cess,
by you will find; Hur - ry - ing on - ward, o'er life's high-way,

Thousands be - fore you have made the test; So their ex - am - ple
Sor - row, and sad - ness, or hap - pi - ness; Trust- ed and hon - ored,
You may for - get and go far a - stray; Now is the time, ere

should be your guide; Scorn not to heed it; cast off your pride;
doubt - ed, and then Passed by un - no - ticed, lost a - mong men;
it be too late; Why un - de - cid - ed? don't trust to fate;

By permission.

On - ly one way, then, is there for thee: Up- ward or down - ward,
Glo - ri - ous man-hood wreck'd in life's sea; Up- ward or down - ward,
In the bright fu - ture, wait- ing for thee; Up- ward or down - ward,

CHORUS.

which shall it be? Flee from the wine- cup; turn from the glass:
which shall it be?
which shall it be?

Noth - ing but wa - ter your lips should pass; Will you be slaves or

will you be free? Up - ward or down-ward, which shall it be?

Tramp, Tramp, Tramp.

MARY T. LATHROP.   J. H. TENNEY.

1. Tramp, tramp, tramp, in the drunkard's way, March the feet of a mil-lion men;
2. Tramp, tramp, tramp, to a drunkard's doom, Out of boy-hood pure and fair,
3. Tramp, tramp, tramp, till a drunkard's grave Hides the bro-ken life of shame;

If none shall pit-y none shall save, Where will the march they are making end?
O - ver the tho'ts of love and home, Past the restraint of a mother's pray'r;
The souls that Je-sus died to save, Meeting an end that we dare not name.

Young and strong with the old are there, In woeful ranks as they hur-ry past,
On-ward swift to a drunkard's crime, O - ver the plea of the wife and child,
God help all! there's a cross to bear, And work to do for the might-y throng;

With not a mo-ment to think or care, What is the fate that comes at last.
And o'er the ho-li-est ties of time, Rea-son dethron'd, the soul gone wild.
God gives us strength, till toil and pray'r Ends by and by in the vic-tor's song.

The Army of the Wine-King. 21

MRS. A. L. DAVISON.   J. H. ROSECRANS.

1. { 1st *Voice*. Watchman, on   the mountain standing,   Gaz-ing o - ver all the
   { 2d *Voice*. Lo, an en -   e - my is com-ing!   Come to bat - tle now with
2. { 1st *Voice*. Knowest thou   from whence they're coming, From the land,   or from the
   { 2d *Voice*. From the in - land   they are com-ing,   And their ban- ners are blood-
3. { 1st *Voice*. Ah! we know   these blood-red ban-ners;   Long they've waved above our
   { 2d *Voice*. 'Tis the Wine-King's hosts that com- eth;   Faith-ful hearts,   be wise, be

land, What is there   of good or e - vil? Tell us, we   of thee demand. }
thee; Light the fires   up- on the hill-tops; Marshal all   the brave and true. }
sea?   Of what na - tion are their banners? Tell us, we of   thee   demand. }
red;   When they pass, the earth is la - den With the dy - ing and   the dead. }
land; Long we've seen our lov'd ones falling. Stricken by that cru - el band. }
strong, And, remember'ring all the fal- len, Vow to right this fear- ful wrong. }

CHORUS.

To arms!   To arms!   The foe!   The foe!   Gird
   To arms!   To arms!   The foe!   The foe!

on, O hearts of oak! The battle sword of God and truth, And heav'n direct each stroke.

From "The Beauty," by permission.

A Foe in the Land.

MRS. L. H. WASHINGTON.　　　　　J. W. BISCHOFF.

Moderato.

•1. There's an en - e - my at band; Shall we for - ward march or
2. 'Tis a foe with smil- ing face, Who with win - some, charm-ing
3. Ral - ly for that no - ble son: Ral - ly for the cher-ished
4. For - ward march with-out de - lay, Or the foe may win the

stand, While there is with-in our land a dead- ly foe? One that
grace, Binds his vic - tim first, with frailest silk-en band; But his
one Up - on whom the light and joy of life de - pend; Are thy
day; He is rais - ing new recruits on ev' - ry hand; Ral- ly

char-ges on the soul, Lurk - ing in the spark- ling bowl, Lead - ing
pow - er will in-crease; He will ban - ish joy and peace, As he
treas-ures all se- cure? Hast thou noth- ing to en - dure? Ral - ly
with the bat - tle - cry, "Those we love may sure - ly die If we

From "Crystal Songs," by permission.

on   to   fol - ly, ru - in, crime, and   war.
holds with fa - tal grasp aud   i - rou hand.
then, with ten - der hoart for neigh - bor, friend.
do   not rout the foe with - iu the   land."

CHORUS.
Con Spirito.

On,   on,   on, the foe is march - ing! Bear-ing to death a might-y
* Shout, shout, shout, the boys are turn - ing! Cheer up, ye lov'd ones, they will

throng;   Let us ral - ly at the call, Ral - ly brave - ly, one and
come,   With a heart, true, warm, and light, And a step that says, "All

all,   God is lend - ing in the bat - tle 'gainst the wrong.
right!" Bring-ing glad - ness to each well be - lov - ed home.

* These words for last time.

24 Drink Ye from the Crystal Fountain.

LIZZIE ASHBACH.   J. H. KURZENKNABE.

1. Drink ye from the crys - tal foun-tain, Of   the wa - ter fresh and clear;
2. Beau - ti - ful and spark-ling wa - ter, Pure and fresh and ev - er free;
3. Giv - en un - to us   iu mer - cy, For our way thro' life to cheer;
4. Flow- ing free for ev - 'ry na - tion; Giv - en pure to ev - 'ry clime;
5. Nev - er touch the sparkling poi - son Lest its curs - es thee be - fall;

D. C. Drink ye from the crys - tal fount- ain, Of the wa - ter fresh and clear;

Fine.

Not a poi - son here is flow - ing: Here's no venomed sting to fear.
Drink of heav - en's own pure fountain, Flow -ing on for you and me.
And we thank thee, Heav'nly Fa - ther. For the wa - ter sweet and clear.
Bet - ter than the li - quid poi - son Which is tak - en from the vine.
Here's your health to sparkling wa - ter, Flow- ing pure and free to all.

Not a poi - son there is flowing; There's no venomed sting to fear.

CHORUS.

Turn a- way from wine's temptation; Nev - er let   its taste al- lure;

D.C.

Drink of hea -ven's crys - tal nec - tar, Sparkling, clear, and pure; Go,

By permission.

REV. J. B. ATCHISON.   W. S. MARSHALL.

1. Who hath sor-row? who hath woe? They who dare not answer "No!"
2. Who hath babblings? who hath strife? He who leads a drunkard's life;
3. Who hath wounds without a cause? He who breaks God's ho-ly laws;
4. Who hath red-ness in the eyes? Who brings pov-er-ty and sighs
5. Touch not, taste not, han-dle not; Wine will make a dark, dark blot;

They whose feet to sin in-cline; They who tar-ry long at wine.
He who scorns the Lord di-vine; He who goes to seek mix'd wine.
He whose lov'd ones weep and pine While he tar-ries at the wine.
In-to homes al-most di-vine? They who tar-ry at the wine.
Like an ad-der it will sting, And at last to ru-in bring.

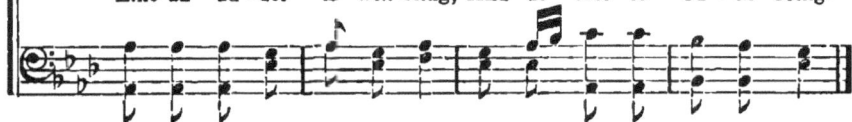

CHORUS.

They who tar-ry at the wine-cup, They who tar-ry at the wine-cup,

They who tar-ry at the wine-cup; They have sorrow; they have woe.

From Cook's "TEACHERS' and SCHOLARS' QUARTERLY," by permission.

Beware!

FOR MALE VOICES.

J. LAWSON.

J. H. TENNEY.

1. Err - ing friend, be-ware, be - ware! Oth - ers have been shipwrecked
2. Thou- sands on this rock have split, And their cries are sound - ing
3. Haste, my broth -er, save your soul And at once the foe con-

where Fear - less, un - a-larmed you steer; Change your course, the rocks are
yet; Still, un - heed- ing those who've gone, Thousands more are rush - ing
-trol; None but fiends would have you sup Dead - ly poi - son from the

near!.... Halt, be - fore it is too late! Shun the drunkard's aw - ful
on! .... Ev - er- more the cup for - sake; Now a friend - ly warn-ing
cup;.... Let not, then your deathless soul E'er be ru - ined by the

fate; Oh, may it be ne'er for - got! Touch not, taste not, han - dle
take; Oh, es - cape the drunk - ard's lot! Touch not, taste not, han - dle
bowl; Now ac - cept the les - son taught, Touch not, taste not, han - dle

not! Touch not, taste not, han - dle not!
not! Touch not, taste not, han - dle not!
not! Touch not, taste not, han - dle not!

Say "No!"

M. Snyder.

J. H. T.

1. When you are tempted the wine to drink, Pause a mo-ment, my
2. Think of a moth-er's grief and pain; Think of tears that will
3. Think of a man-hood's taint-ed breath; Of the sor-row and
4. Think of lone graves, un-wept, unknown, Hiding the hopes that were
5. Think of the de-mon that fills the bowl, Bring-ing ru-in to

friend, and think! Think of the wrecks on life's o-cean tossed,
fall like rain; Think of her heart and the cru-el blow;
pain and death; Think of the home that is dark with woe;
once your own; Think of lov'd forms in the dust laid low,
life and soul; Think of all this as life's path you go,

Chorus.

All for the failure to count the cost. Answer them "No," Answer them, "No,"
Think of her love, and then answer, "No."
On-ly because you did not say "No."
Who would be here had they answered "No."
And when you're tempted, say, boldly, "No." "No," "No;"

1. When you are tempt-ed, bold-ly say "No," 2. Bold-ly say "No."

National Temperance Song.

Rev. Dwight Williams.

J. H. Tenney.

1. Co-lum-bi - a, fresh as the glow of the morn-ing, And
2. A mon - arch of e - vil, en-throned in his splen - dor. Now
3. Co-lum-bi - a, hast - en! Co - lum - bi - a, speed thee! The

strong in the race of the na-tions to run, A ty - rant is ris-ing; look
hold- eth his rod o'er the land of the free; Arouse thee! arouse thee! with
wide world is wait- ing the shout of the brave; Then rush to the con-flict, and

well to the warn-ing, And guard the dear land of thine own Washington!
God thy de-fend- er, And drive him for-e'er to the depths of the sea!
on- ward God lead ye, Till high on the ramparts our ban - ner shall wave.

Chorus.

Co - lum - bi - a, rise! The God of the skies Looks

ff rall.

down on the strug - gle and hold - eth the prize!

A. W. FRENCH. ·   J. H. T.

1. Yield not to the tempter; Pass by and be free; For yield- ing is
2. Yield not to the tempter; Turn quick ly a - way; Go, min- gle with
3. Yield not to the tempter; Be firm and be true; And God, in your

ru - in And sor - row for thee; Why should you now bar - ter
hon - or In life's bu - sy fray; Fall not from your sta - tion,
weak- ness, Your strength shall re-new; To him your pe - ti - tion

the jew - el of youth, With shame for your honor, And wrong for the truth?
What- ev- er it be; Keep clear from the dan-ger That beck - ons to thee
Send upward a - gain, That you may be ev - er a man a-mong men.

CHORUS.

Yield not to the tempt - er; pass by and be free;

For yield - ing is ru - in and sor - row for thee.

Onward!

MRS. E. W. CHAPMAN.   J. H. TENNEY.

1. " On! " thy brother's blood is cry - ing; " On! " the call rings far and near;
2. Why stand halt- ing all the morn-ing? Hast - en quickly to the work;
3. Hand to hand the bat - tle wag - ing Firmly grasp thy sword and fight;

Orphan's tears and widow's sigh- ing, Plead their breaking hearts to cheer;
On! and well thy part per-form-ing, No al - lot-ted du - ty shirk
In the hot - test toil en - gag - ing, Till you triumph for the right.

CHORUS.

On-ward, onward, onward to the res-cue! For the call rings loud and clear;

rit.

On-ward, onward, onward brother, sister! Shout the watchword; help is near.

Down at the Cross.

E. A. H   REV. J. H. STOCKTON.

1. Down at the cross where my Saviour died, Down where for cleansing from
2. I am so wondrous-ly saved from sin, Je-sus so sweet-ly a-
3. Won-der-ful fount-ain that saves from sin: I am so glad I have
4. Come to the fount-ain, so rich and sweet, Cast thy poor soul at the

sin I cried, There to my heart was the blood ap-plied;
hides with-in; There at the cross he has made me clean;
en-tered in; Here Je-sus saves me and keeps me clean;
Sa-viour's feet; Plunge in to-day and be made com-plete;

CHORUS.

Glo - ry to his name! Glo - ry to his
Glo - ry to his name!
Glo - ry to his name!
Glo - ry to his name!

name!...... Glo - ry to his name!

There to my heart was the blood ap-plied; Glo-ry to his name!

By permission.

She Told him 'Twould be so.

FANNIE J. CROSBY. QUARTET, T. F. SEWARD.

1. 'Tis night; the drunkard sits a-lone; The au-tumn rain-drops fall;
2. There was a time he would have spurn'd The cold and reckless throng,
3. He did not plunge at once in crime, But step by step he trod;
4. He closed his eyes, as if to hide The pres-ent from his sight;

Why does he quail be-neath its glance—That pic-ture on the wall?
Whose mid-night rev-el now he seeks, And where he tar-ries long:
One glass, an-oth-er; then his lips Pro-faned the name of God;
The hours sped on, the storm had passed, The morn-ing sun was bright:

A pale young face; he knows it well, And loved it long a-go;
A mo-ment, when he felt the tear Of deep con-tri-tion flow;
A wreck of all he might have been, A slave to guilt and woe,
They came to rouse him, but the tide Of life had ceased to flow;

But now, Oh, heav'n! he dare not think; She told him 'twould be so;
But conscience seldom whispers now; She told him 'twould be so;
'Till rea-son trembles on its throne; She told him 'twould be so;
They laid him in a stranger's grave; She told him 'twould be so;

She told him 'twould be so.

But now, Oh, heav'n! he dare not think; She told him 'twould be so.
But conscience, etc. She told him 'twould be so.

By permission.

REV. P. S. ORWIG.   NATHAN BARKER.

1 Fight the bat - tle!   fight the bat - tle!   Faith is need - ed
2 Fight the bat - tle!   fight the bat - tle!   Grace and cour - age
3 Fight the bat - tle!   fight the bat - tle!   Though the war be

to be strong; Walls and bul - warks need not check you,
he'll sup - ply; If you firm - ly stand for Je - sus,
hand to hand, We shall see the foe re - treat - ing,

CHORUS.

Christ, the vic - tor, bids you come. Fight the bat - tle!
You shall have a home on high.
Con- quer'd by our no - ble band.

fight the bat - tle! Gird your ar - mor on;....

Fight the bat-tle! Fight the bat -tle! Till you gain the crown.

By permission.

No Surrender.

J. H. TENNEY.

1. Ev - er constant, ev - er true, Let the word be "No sur-
2. Nail the col - ors to the mast, Shout - ing glad - ly "No sur-
3. Con - stant and cou - ra - geous still, Mind, the word is "No sur-

- ren-der!" Bold - ly dare and greatly do. This shall bring us bravely
- ren-der!" Troubles near are all but past; Serve them as you did the
- ren-der!" Bat - tle, tho' it be up hill; Stag - ger not at seeming

through, No surren-der, no sur-ren - der! And tho' fortune's smiles be
last; No surren-der, no sur-ren - der! Tho' the skies be o - ver-
ill; No surren-der, no sur-ren - der! Hope, and thus your hope ful-

few;.... Hope is al - ways spring-ing new, Still in-
cast;.... And up - on the sleet - y blast, Dis - ap-
fil,.... There's a way where there's a will; And the

- spir - ing me and you With a ma - gic "No sur - ren-der!"
point-ments gath - er fast, Beat them off with "No sur - ren-der!"
way all cares to kill Is to give them "No sur - ren-der!"

REFRAIN.

No, no, no, no, no sur-render! No, no, no, no, no sur-ren-der!

God will Help you through,

E. A. HOFFMAN. J. H. T.

1. Broth-er, be thou faith - ful; Brother, be thou true;
2. Tho' your foes be man - y, And your help - ers few,
3. You may feel your weak - ness, But your way pur - sue;
4. Un - der all tempt - a - tion Be thou brave and true:

You need not fight the fight a - lone; God will help you through.
Be not dis - cour - aged, nor des - pair; God will help you through.
In weak - ness God will be your strength; He will help you through.
O trust in his al - might-y arm; He will help you through.

D.S. You need not fight the fight a - lone, God will help you through.

CHORUS. D.S.

God will help you through; Yes, God will help you through.

Copyright, 1879, by OLIVER DITSON & Co.

Hallelujah! Marching On.

C. H. GABRIEL.   J. H. TENNEY.

1. We are a loy - al, earn - est band, And fight - ing for the
2. The hosts of sin are press - ing hard, But nev - er will we
3. We float our ban - ner in the breeze, And shout our Lead- er's

right; And we are marching on to war With ar - mor shin- ing bright;
yield; We'll nev - er lay the ar - mor by, Nor quit the bat - tle field;
name; Re - joic- ing, we will march and sing His hon - ors to pro-claim;

The foes are ma - ny we shall meet That seek to bar our
We have a Cap - tain firm and true; He bids us all be
And when in bat - tle we shall fall, a crown of life he'll

way, But with a lead - er such as ours, We'll sure-ly gain the day.
strong, And fight for him with all our might, Al - tho' the strife be long.
give, And ev -'ry val - iant sol- dier here, In heav'n with Christ shall live.

Copyright, 1879, by OLIVER DITSON & Co.

CHORUS.

Hal - le - lu - jah! march - ing on,   With our
march - ing   on,

ban - ner proud - ly bor ne;   In the work we have be-
ban - ner proud- ly borne;

- gun; The vic - t'ry we will win; Je - sus leads us to the
leads us

fight   For the good, the true, and right,   And, with
to the fight   the true, and right,

ar - mor shin - ing bright, We'll con - quer ev - 'ry sin.

38 The Prodigal Coming Home.

" And he arose and came to his father."—Luke xv: 10.

REV. H. B HARTZLER.   E. S. LORENZ.

1. In the wilds of sin a wea-ry soul, a-stray From the
2. But he heard a voice in ten-der mer-cy say, "Sin-ner,
3 Com-ing home, all faint and hun-gry and a-thirst, To the
4. Com-ing home, to seek a bless-ed mer-cy-seat, With a

home of love had gone; Like a poor lost lamb, he
come; why long-er stray?" And he comes, he comes, a-
feast of love and peace; Com-ing home, by all the
load of guilt and shame, And a con-trite heart, to

wandered far a-way, In his grief and woe a-lone....
long the homeward way; Com-ing home no more to stray.
woe of sin ac-curst, To re-ceive a quick re-lease.
lay at Je-sus' feet, In the faith of his dear name.

CHORUS.

Yes, the prod-i-gal's coming home, coming home, no more to roam, He is

wea-ry of wan-d'ring far a-way from home; He is

From " HEAVENLY CAROLS," by permission.

seeking the Father's face; he is long - ing for his grace; Yes, the

prod - i - gal's com - ing home, com - ing home................
com - ing home.

Brother, Go.

J. H. T.

1. Broth - er, go To the high and to the low, To the
2. Broth - er, go With the mes - sage all men need; Go to
3. Fly, fly, fly, For time hast - ens; death is nigh; Haste o'er

wea - ry, who are sigh - ing; To the crush'd ones, faint with crying; To poor
ev' - ry land and na - tion; Go to ev - 'ry class and sta - tion; Spread the
mount and plain and val - ley, Thro' each highway, by -way, al - ley; All man-

souls with burdens dy - ing; Go, and tell ev -'ry one Christ bids them come.
gra - cious in - vi -ta - tion, Tell them Christ's blessed call Ex-tends to all.
kind to Je - sus ral - ly, For he calls them to-day; Let none de - lay.

.Look Aloft.

MAJ. THEO. I. ECKERSON.   JNO. R. SWENEY.

1. When the heart has grown sick of the world's sin and blight, When
2. Should slan - der as - sail you, or trou - bles a - rise, Stand
3. When bil - lows of an - guish, with mer - ci - less shock, Roll

hope seems de - part - ing, and friends have grown old', Look a-
firm to your ban - ner thro' sor - row and shame; Look a-
fierce - ly, aud faith al - most drowns in the wave, Look a-

loft, look a - loft, look a - loft, Look a - loft to the rain - bow so
loft, look a - loft, look a - loft, Look a - loft to your home in the
loft, look a - loft, look a - loft, Look a - loft to the Cross and the

bright, God's mes - sage of peace set in pur - ple and gold.
skies, For he who re - deem'd you once suf - fered the same.
Rock, To the Sa - viour who stands ev - er read - y to save.

CHORUS.
Look a - loft, look a - loft Look a-
look a - loft, look a - loft,
loft; be not dismayed, For the sweet prom-ise
Look a - loft
giv - en us nev - er shall fail; With hope for an an - chor, let
none be a - fraid; Look a - loft, Look a-
look a - loft,
loft, look a - loft, look a - loft, and we'll ride on the gale.

Dash the Wine-Cup Away.

W. H. BURLEIGH.   E. ROBERTS.

1. Dash the wine-cup a-way, tho' its spar-kle shall be   More
2. Wher-ev-er the cup of con-fu-sion is poured, In the
3. Then ral-ly, then ral-ly, ye wise and ye good;   Come

bright than the gems that lie hid in the sea; For a sy-ren, un-
cel-lar of want, or at lux-u-ry's board, From pal-ace and
up in your strength, and roll back the dark flood, Ere your trea-sures are

seen by thine eye, lurk-eth there, Who would lure thee thro' plea-sure to
cot-tage, from hov-el and hall,   A   wail go-eth up to the
wrecked in its des-o-late path, As it sweeps o'er your homes in its

CHORUS.

want and despair.   Then dash, dash the wine-cup; 'tis death to de-
Fath-er of all.
ter-ror and wrath.

lay; Be a man, while you can; dash the wine-cup a-way!

By permission.

Jesus Saves.

Rev. W. H. Burrell.   W. J. Kirkpatrick.

1. Oh, this ut - ter- most sal - va - tion! Spread the news thro'-out cre-
2. Plung'd beneath this crim - son fount-ain, O - pened in God's ho - ly
3. Now I see the fount - ain flow-ing, Life and bliss on me be-
4. Oh, the rap-ture! Oh, the glo - ry! Wrought in me by this old
5. When beyond death's roll- ing riv - er, In that bless - ed bright for-

- a - tion, Je-sus saves from sin's con - ta - gion, Je- sus saves, Je- sus saves!
mountain, Thrills my soul with sweet e-mo - tion, Je- sus saves, Je- sus saves!
stow- ing; Now my heart with love is glow - ing, Je- sus saves, Je- sus saves!
sto - ry; Brightest vis-ions rise be - fore me; Je- sus saves, Je- sus saves!
ev - er, This blest song shall ech-o ev - er, Je- sus saves, Je- sus saves!

CHORUS.

Je - sus saves me; glo - ry, glo - ry! Oh, the wondrous

won - drous sto - ry! Je - sus saves. Je - sus saves, Je - sus saves!

Copyright, 1879, by Oliver Ditson & Co.

44   Look on the Bright Side.

W. G. BURNHAM.   J. H. T.

Allegretto.

1. There's sunshine and joy up - on earth, my good friend, Tho' it
2. Then when he shall leave you and go on his way, He may
3. Oh! life would be hap - pier to all, if we knew The

seems full of dark-ness and sor - row, And the storm-clouds which shadow the
feel his heart warm'd by your bright-ness, And strengthen'd to bear well his
fol - ly and sin of complain - ing, For tho' sometimes its comforts seem

light of to-day May not sha-dow the light of to-mor - row.
cross-es and pains, With a soul ris-ing up in its bright - ness.
all to have fled, Yet great blessings are al-ways re-main - ing.

CHORUS.

Oh look on the bright side, and not on the dark; Make the

best of the troubles you're meet-ing; And with heart that is hopeful, grasp

warm-ly the hand Which your neighbor ex-tends with a greet-ing.

In God We Trust.

E. A. HOFFMAN.

J. H. T.

Quick and Spirited.

1. In God we trust! He is our sure De-fence; He shields us
2. In God we trust! He is a sol-id Rock, Un-moved and
3. In God we trust! He is our Help-er now; We pay to

with His own om-nip-o-tence. In God we trust,
firm A-gainst all earth-ly shock. In God we
him Our hum-ble, sol-emn vow.

CHORUS.

In God we trust! For help and strength, In God we trust!
trust! In God we trust! For help and strength,

By permission.

Rouse thee, Brother.

" Therefore let us not sleep as do others."—1 Thess. v : 6.

MRS. H. A. FOSTER.   J. H. TENNEY.

1. Rouse thee, broth-er, from thy slum- ber; 'Tis the noon of day;
2. Join the columns, strong and stea - dy, Mov - ing on the foe;
3. Make no truce; the land is ly - ing 'Neath the curse of rum;

Slug-gards in re - pose out-num-ber Earn - est souls to - day.
Heart be true, and hand be read- y For the fin - al blow.
Wom - en pray - ing, or - phans cry- ing, Jus - tice faint and dumb;

Thou art keep - er of thy neigh- bor, Yet dost i - dly dream;
Lift the pure, white ban - ner proud - ly; Guard it with thy might;
Storm the le - gal ram- parts, shield- ing Haunts of shame and sin;

Rouse, and get thee to the la - bor Of this hour su - preme.
Shout a - long the line, and loud - ly, "God is with the right!"
Give no quar - ter, know no yield - ing, And the right shall win.

CHORUS.

Rouse ye, sons and broth - ers! Sleep not as do oth - ers!

"To the front!" heed the call; Form in the line; for - ward all!

Anchored Fast.

REV. W. P. BREED. J. H. TENNEY.

1. Tossing on the bil-low, Rock - ing in the blast, Fainting on the pil - low,
2. Skies all clad in sa- ble, Storm-clouds scudding past, Clinging to the ca - ble,
3. Gone each earthly treasure, Cut a-way each mast, Vanish'd earthly pleasure,

CHORUS.

Verging toward the last. While the tem - pest ra - ges, To the Rock of.
I am anchored fast.
Still I'm anchored fast.

1.
A - ges I am anchored fast,

2.
I am anchored fast.

Do they Pray for me Home?

J. H. TENNEY.

1. Do they pray for me at home? Do they ev - er pray for me
2. Do they pray for me at home When the sum-mer birds ap-pear?
3. Do they pray for me at home When the winds of win - ter blow?

When I ride the dark sea foam, When I cross the storm - y sea?
Do they pray for me the while, That my path may be less drear?
Do they pray for me with love As they watch the win - ter's snow?

Oh! how oft in for-eign lands, As I see the bend-ed knee,
At the home of ear - ly youth, Do they place the va - cant chair,
In the sea - son's chil -ly cold. Are their hearts for me still warm?

Comes the tho't at twi-light hour, Do they ev - er pray for me?
Where my heart so oft re - turns, To the lov'd ones gathered there?
Am I cherished as of old Thro' the beat- ing of the storm?

REFRAIN.

Do they ev - er, do they ev- er, Do they ev - er pray for me at home?

From "SHINING LIGHT," by permission.

Do they ev-er, do they ev-er, Do they ev-er pray for me at home?

Lo, the Morning Dawneth.

J. E. HALL.   CHAS. H. GABRIEL.

1. Lo, the morning dawneth, broth-er! Glad the news comes from all lands;
2. Lift your eyes to see the glo-ry Mark-ing the Mes-si-ah's reign;
3. Hark! I hear the glad song ring-ing; Oh, what mu-sic 'tis to hear!
4. Sin's dark night now yields to morn-ing; Bright the day-star's beams a-rise,

Fine.

Hosts of hosts to Je-sus turn-ing, Breaking loose from Sa-tan's bands.
Look! the ban-ner high is wav-ing, These words bearing, "Peace proclaim."
Vic-to-ry for Zi-on turn-ing, Rends the sky with cheer on cheer.
Fill-ing hill-top, plain and val-ley, And the blue-arched, vaulted skies.

D. S. Hosts of hosts to Je-sus turn-ing, Break-ing loose from Satan's bands.

CHORUS. *ff*   *D.S.*

Morn-ing dawn-eth, morning dawneth; Glad the news comes from all lands;

Mother is Dead.

QUARTET.

Words and Music by E. A. HOFFMAN.

Expressivo.

1. Moth-er is dead, and I am a-lone. Friendless, un-loved, un-
2. Home was so bright, so cheer-ful and glad, Till fath-er drank, and
3. Moth-er grew pale, and broke her poor heart; Oh, how I wept to

cared for, un-known; Fath-er a-bove! come in thy love,
made our hearts sad; Sor-row and pain came to us then,
see her de-part! Now she is gone; I am a-lone;

Take me to moth-er in heav-en a-bove; Fath-er a-bove!
Ne'er could we smile or be hap-py a-gain: Sor-row and pain
No one to pit-y; I'm homeless unknown; Now she is gone!

come in thy love, Take me to moth-er in heav-en a-bove.
came to us then; Ne'er could we smile or be hap-py a-gain.
I am a-lone; No one to pit-y; I'm homeless, unknown.

4 Life is so dark since mother is dead;
It is so hard to beg for my bread:
No one for months on me has smiled;
Pity and pray for the poor drunkard's
child!

5 Merciful God, O send in thy love,
From thy bright throne in heaven
above,

Angels to win back from his sin
My wretched father to virtue again!

6 Temperance men, Oh, do you not think
You can win back my father from
drink?
Tell him his child wanders alone,
Shelterless, homeless, unpitied, un-
known!

See the Light Advancing.

MRS. E. W. CHAPMAN.　　　　　　　　　　　　　　　J. H. T.

1. See the light advancing; East and west it gleams, Gilding ev - 'ry mo ntain,
2. An - gel eyes are watching Those who go a- stray; Help us lead them, Father,
3. We will press on bravely Till the truth prevails; He who fights with Jesus

Glist'ning on the streams; With its brilliance scatt'ring Sunbeams on the sea,
In the nar - row way; With a love un- tir - ing, Clasping hand in hand,
Nev - er, nev - er fails; We will meet the foe - man, Fill'd with courage true,

CHORUS.

Bidding shades of er - ror From our na - tion flee. See the light advancing;
We will guide them homeward To the bet - ter land.
And with Christ as Captain, Fight the bat -tle through.

Truth is marching on; God will give us vic - t'ry Thro' his bless- ed Son.

Never say Fail.

ALDINE S. KIEFFER

1. Keep work - ing; 'tis wis - er than sit - ting a - side And
2. With eyes ev - er o - pen, a tongue that's not dumb, A
3. In life's ro - sy morn - ing, in man-hood's fair pride, Let

dreaming and sigh-ing and waiting the tide: In life's earnest bat - tle they
heart that to sor-row will nev-er succumb, You bat - tle and conquer, tho'
this be your mot- to, your footsteps to guide, "In storm and in sunshine, what-

on - ly pre- vail Who dai - ly march onward, and nev - er say fail!
thousands as - sail; How strong and how migh-ty who nev - er say fail!
ev - er as - sail, I'll on-ward and conquer, and nev - er say fail!"

CHORUS.

Nev- er, oh, nev - er say fail!...... Nev- er, oh, nev - er say
oh, nev-er say fail! oh,

fail! In life's earnest bat - tle, they on - ly pre- vail Who
nev-er say fail!

By permission.

nev - - - er, no   nev - - - er say   fail!
nev - er, no nev - er, no   nev - er, no nev - er say   fail!

Dare to do Right.

E. A. HOFFMAN.   WEBER.

1. When   the wine - cup   is   of - fered, All spark-ling and fair,
2. Come   and join . us, com - pan - ions, U - nite with our band;
3. Well   we know that your cour - age Will of - ten be tried,

Nei - ther touch it nor taste it, For death lin - gers there.
Come; in love and in friend-ship We of - fer our hand.
But the bless - ed Re - deem - er Will stand by your side.

No - bly stand by your man-hood; Re - sist it with might;
If the temp - ter as - sails you, Be strong in the fight,
He has promised to help you, And pledged you his might;

Do not yield to temp - ta - tion But dare to do right.
For the Sa - viour will help you; Then dare to do right.
Then be bold and cou - ra - geous, And dare to do right.

All my Life Long.

JOSEPHINE POLLARD.

Arranged by J. H. T.

1. All my life long have my steps been at-tend-ed Sure-ly by
2. All in the dark would I be, and un-cer-tain Whith-er to
3. He will not wea-ry, oh, bless-ed as-sur-ance! In-fi-nite

One who re-gard-ed my ways; Ten-der-ly watch'd o-ver,
go, but for One at my side, Who from the fu-ture re-
love will the fi-nite out-last; But for my heav-en-ly

sweet-ly be-friended, Blessings have followed my nights and my days.
moves the dim curtain, See-ing the glo-ry to mortals de-nied.
Father's as-sur-ance, In-to the depths of de-spair I were cast.

CHORUS.

Tears have been quench'd in the sun - shine of glad - ness,
No oth - er friend could so pa - tient - ly lead me;
This is my star in a mid - night of sor - row,

Au - thems of sor - row been turned in - to song;
No oth - er friend prove so faith - ful and true;
This is my re - fuge, my strength, and my song;

An - gels have guard - ed the gate - ways of sad - ness,
With au - gels' food He has prom - ised to feed me,
"Earth is to - day, but there's hea - ven to - mor - row,

Sum - mer and win - ter, yea, all my life long.
Who has be- friend - ed me all my life long.
And He will guide me yea, all my life long."

56

"Fall In."

F. L. B.

F. L. BRISTOW.

1. Wea - ry of the Mas-ter's fight, Sleep - ing all the day and night?
2. Straggling from the Lord's command, Seek - ing pleas - ures of the land?
3. Murm'ring, fight-ing for the right, Heav -en's por - tals just in sight?

Sleeping? sleep-ing? Dan - gers lurk - ing nigh? Up, ye wea- ry sol - diers!
Wand'ring? straggling? Tempters round thee lie? Ral - ly, straggling sol - diers!
Murm'ring? murm'ring? With a dole - ful sigh? List, ye murm'ring sol - diers!

Hear your val - iant Cap- tain's cry—"Fall in! Press on! Vic- t'ry by and by!"
Hear your val - iant Cap- tain's cry—"Fall in! Press on! Vic- t'ry by and by!"
Hear your val - iant Cap- tain's cry—"Fall in! Press on! Vic- t'ry by and by!"

CHORUS.

Sa - tan comes, with might - y hosts, And des - o - lates the land;

D.S.

Sow - ing seeds of sor - row and des - pair on ev - 'ry hand.

From "SONGS OF GRATITUDE," by permission.

Let me Come to Thee.

E. A. HOFFMAN.　　　　　　　　　　　　J. H. TENNEY.

1. In the wil - derness of sin, Far a- way from home, I, a lone - ly
2. I am des - ti-tute of peace; Take me in thy arms, Bear me to thy
3. Lead the wea- ry prod-i - gal In the nar- row way; Let me, O Re-

wan- der - er, In the darkness roam; Heav -y are the shad - ows
ten - der fold, Safe from all a - larms; Calm up - on thy bo - som,
- deem- er mine! Nev - er from thee stray; Par- don all my sin - ning;

That en - cir - cle me; Je-sus, precious Sa- viour, Let me come to thee!
Kind - ly shel-ter me; Je-sus, precious Sa- viour, Let me come to thee!
Shield and bless thou me; Je-sus, precious Sa- viour, Let me come to thee!

CHORUS.

Je - sus, Sa - viour, Let me come to thee!
Je - sus let me come to thee! Sa - - viour, let me come to

Pre - cious Sa - viour, Let me come to thee!
thee! Precious Sa-viour, let me come to thee!

From "SONGS OF FAITH," by permission.

Jesus and Victory!

E. A. H.

E. A. HOFFMAN.

1. On, val - iant sol- diers of Christ, our King! On, till the world to his
2. On, till the mil- lions shall heed the call! On, till the king- doms of
3. On, ye his sol- diers, in close ar - ray! On, and be firm, till the

feet you bring! On, let the war - cry in tri - umph ring,
sin shall fall! On, till the king -dom shall rule o'er all!
foe gives way! On, we are gain - ing for Christ the day!

CHORUS.

"Je - sus and vic - to - ry!" On, val -iant sol - diers of the
"Je - sus and vic - to - ry!"
"Je - sus and vic - to - ry!"

cross, Fol - low your Lord and King;
on, on! on! on!

On, till the glad notes of vic - to - ry Loud thro' the wel - kin ring.

By permission.

Falling into Line.

MRS. E. C. ELLSWORTH.   J. H. TENNEY.

1. Fall- ing in - to line, boys, Fall- ing in   to - day;   Read - y when   the
2. Fill- ing up   the ranks, boys, Ev - 'ry one in place,   Read - y for   the
3. Je - sus is   for right, boys; Right shall never fail;   Nev - er quit   the

or - der comes, Read-y to   o - bey;   Ar - mor must be bright, boys;
bat - tle fierce, Quick the foe to face; Stand-ing for   the right, boys,
field,   my boys, Till the right pre-vail; Hear the shout   go up,   boys,

Let the steel be true, For the coming vic - to - ry May depend on you.
Put- ing down the wrong, Helping all the wea-ry ones, Mak-ing man -y strong.
Triumph must be near; 'Tis our com-ing victory; Cheer then, comrades, cheer!

CHORUS.

Fall- ing in - to line, boys, Fall - ing in to- day;   Read - y when the

1.
or - der comes, Read - y to   o - bey,
2.
Read - y to   o - bey.

Copyright, 1879, by OLIVER DITSON & Co.

60 # Go, Feel what I have Felt.

QUARTET.

A young lady of New York was in the habit of writing on the subject of Temperance. Her writing was so full of pathos, and evinced such deep emotion of soul, that a friend of hers accused her of being a maniac on the subject of Temperance, whereupon she wrote this hymn.

E. A. H.

1. Go, feel what I have felt; Go, bear what I have borne; Sink
2. Go, weep as I have wept O'er a lov'd fa-ther's fall; See
3. Go to my mother's side, And her crushed bo- som cheer; Thine
4. Go, hear and see and know All that my soul hath known. Then

'neath a blow a fa-ther dealt, And the cold world's proud scorn; Then suffer
ev- 'ry promised bless-ing swept, Youth's sweetness turn'd to gall, Life's fading
own deep woe and anguish hide And wipe the bit- ter tear; Mark her worn
look up - on the wine-cup's glow, See if it can a-tone; Think if its

on from year to year, Thy sole re - lief the scorch-ing tear.
powers strew'd all the way That bro't me up to wom- an's day.
frame and with- ered brow, The gray that streaks her dark hair now.
fla - vor you will try, When all pro- claim, 'tis drink and die.

CHORUS.

Then you'll renounce the cup, And haste to give it up; You'll

set your will firm as the steel, And fight with an un-

Copyright, 1879, by Oliver Ditson & Co

daunt- ed zeal, A- gainst the bit - ter cup The bit - ter, bit- ter cup.

Jesus, Plead for Me.

J. H. TENNEY.

1. When by sin and guilt o'er - ta - ken, Sinks my heart, of all for-
2. When the way is rough and drear - y, And the feet are worn and
3. When the pulse of life is fail - ing, Hu - man aid all un - a-

- sa - ken, Je - sus, plead for me; When no lips my cause is
wea - ry, Je - sus, plead for me; When the tempt - er mocks my
vail - ing, Je - sus, plead for me; Till I pass thro' heaven's own

plead -ing, And my soul lies pierc'd and bleed-ing, Je- sus, plead for me!
sor- row, Whispers," You will fall to - mor-row," Je- sus, plead for me!
por - tal, Reach those joys which are im - mor - tal, Je- sus, plead for me!

62 Raise a Song.

E. A. HOFFMAN.   CHAS. H. GABRIEL.

1. Hal - le - lu - jah! raise a song For the tri -umph o- ver wrong; Let the
2. Hal - le - lu - jah! in His might We have struggled for the right, Till we
3. Friends of Je - sus, on-ward move! For the God of truth and love, Who is

ech- oes roll a - long Till in each vale and lea Ev - 'ry tongue shall catch the
conquered in the fight, And the vic-t'ry was won; Now we shout, in grate- ful
thron'd in light a - bove, Asks you now to be true; Ral - ly to his firm com-

strain, And re- ech- o it a-gain, O - ver mountain, hill and plain, To the
lays, Songs of glad.exult-ent praise; To the heav'ns our voi- ces raise To the
-mand; Take the battle-sword in hand; From yon fair,im-mor- tal land He is

CHORUS.

borders of the sea. Hal - le - lu- jah! swell the song For the triumph o - ver
High and Holy One.
looking down on you.

wrong; Peal the lays o'er land and sea: God has gained the vic - to - ry!

Copyright, 1879, by OLIVER DITSON & Co.

Clinging to the Cross.

DR. T. C UPHAM.   J. H. TENNEY.

1. O   Fa - ther! let me bear the cross, Make it   my dai - ly
2. Take house and lands and earth - ly fame, To   all   I am   re-
3. I   know   it costs me man - y tears, But they   are tears of

food, Tho' with it thou dost send the loss Of ev' - ry earth-ly good.
-signed. But let   me make one earnest claim, Leave, leave the cross be-hind.
bliss; And moments there outweigh the years Of self - ish hap - pi - ness.

CHORUS.

I am cling-ing to the cross, I am clinging to the cross; Yes, I'm

cling - ing   to   the cross, I am clinging to the cross, I am
cling - ing, cling - ing

cling - ing to the cross, Yes, I'm cling - ing to the cross.

From "SONGS OF JOY," by permission.

We're Coming.

W. U. BUTCHER.

1. We're com - ing, we're com - ing, the fear - less and free! Like the
2. We're com - ing, we're com - ing, with ban - ners unfurled! And our
3. A - rouse ye, brave hearts! to the res - cue come on! Old King

winds of the des - ert, the waves of the sea; True
mot - to is "Free - dom"; our coun - try, the world; Our
Al - co - hol's ar - my we'll sure - ly put down; He's

sons of our sires, who did bat - tle of yore, When the
watch - word is " Temperance "; let Bac - chus be - ware, For the
slaugh-tered his thou - sands, but now he must yield, For our

foe's haugh - ty ty - rants ran wild on our shore.
pledge or our ar - my will bring him de - spair.
le - gion has ris - en, and ta - ken the field.

CHORUS.

We're com - ing, we're com - ing, from mountain, height and glen, With

By permission.

will - ing hearts to bat - tle for lib - er - ty a - gain; Then

raise we the ban - ner, and ne'er the con- quest yield Till the

ar - my of King Al - co - hol is driv - en from the field.

Mourn for Them.

FOR MALE VOICES   J. H. TENNEY.

1. Mourn for the thousands slain, The youth - ful and the strong;
2. Mourn for the tar - nished gem, For rea - son's light di - vine;
3. Mourn for the lost, but call, Call to the strong, the free;
4. Mourn for the lost, but pray, Pray to our Lord a - bove,

Mourn for the wine-cup's fear-ful reign, And the de - lud - ed throng.
Quench'd from the soul's bright di - a - dem, Where God hath bid it shine.
Rouse them to shun the dread-ful fall, And to the ref - uge flee.
To break the fell de - stroy-er's sway, And show his sav - ing love.

Dear Mother, Cease your Weeping.

Nannette, whose father was a drunkard, seeing the tears of sorrow trickling down her mother's wan cheeks, threw her arms tenderly around her, imprinted a kiss upon her saddened brow, and said, "Dear mother, cease your weeping; we'll trust in God, and be kind to father; perhaps he will grow kind to us again."

E. A. H.   E. A. HOFFMAN.

1. Dear moth - er, cease your wea - ry weep - ing,
2. The sad - den'd years are fast re - ced - ing,
3. Then bear in pa - tient, sweet sub - mis - sion,

For it pains me so   To see the tears of anguish
And the bet - ter day,   With quick - ened pace is hith - er
All your grief and pain;   Per - haps if we are kind to

By permission.

steal - ing A - down the cheeks where joy should glow.
speed - ing, When Christ shall wipe your tears a - way;
fa - ther, He will grow kind to us a - gain.

I know that fa - ther is un - gen - tle; I know be
For soon will come the gold- en mor - row, When you shall
We'll trust in God, my dear-est moth - er, He al - ways

rit.

is not kind and true......... But trust in God, my dear - est
roam yon E - den plain,...... And nev - er know an oth - er
do - eth what is best;...... We'll faith - ful - ly per-form our

68 Dear Mother, Cease your Weeping. Concluded.

moth - er, And he will be a friend to you.
sor - row, Dear moth - er, you'll be hap - py then.
du - ty, And leave to Je - sus all the rest.

CHORUS.

Oh, moth - er, moth - er!
dear moth - er, dear moth - er!

Pa - tient be a few more years; Oh, moth- er, Oh,
dear moth - er,

Repeat pp

moth - er!............ Cease your flow -ing, flow-ing tears.
dear moth -er!

T. HASTINGS.

E. A. PERKINS.

With marked accent.

1. Give me a draught from the crys - tal spring When the burn-ing
2. Give me a draught from the crys - tal spring When the win - try

sun is high, When the rocks and the woods their shadows fling, And the
winds are gone, When the flow'rs are in bloom, and the echoes ring From the

pearls and peb - bles lie. Give me a draught from the crys - tal
woods or flow - 'ry lawn. Give me a draught from the crys - tal

spring When the cool - ing breez-es blow, When the leaves of the
spring When the rip' - ning fruits ap - pear, When a drink from its

trees are with - er - ing From the frost or the flee - cy snow.
pure and cool - ing stream Shall the hearts of the reap-ers cheer.

By permission of FILLMORE BROS.

Sow ye Beside all Waters.

J. H. TENNEY.

Con espressione.

1. Sow ye be-side all wa - ters, Where the dews of heav'n may
2. Sow, tho' the rocks re - pel thee, In its cold and ster - ile

fall; . Ye shall reap, if ye be not wea - ry,
pride; Some cleft may there yet be riv - en,

For the Spirit breathes o'er all. Sow, tho' the thorns may
Where the lit - tle seed may hide. Fear not, tho' some will

wouud thee, One wore the thorns for thee;
flour - ish, And tho' the trees a - bound;

And tho' the cold world scorn thee, Still patient and hope-ful be.
"Like willows, by the wa - ters," Will the scattered grain be found.

CHORUS.

Sow ye beside all wa-ters.Where the dew of heav'n may fall; Ye shall

reap if ye be not wea- ry, For the Spir - it breathes o'er all.

O, Hark to the Stirring Summons!

J. H. T.

1. O hark to the stir - ring sum - mons, "Ye chil - dren of God, a-
2. Then up and at once to the con - flict! 'Tis base - ness to stand a-
3. Re - joice! but with heart's in ten sion; Re - joice! but with chastened

-wake! Ye champions of truth be read - y Your place in the ranks to
part; 'Tis trea - son to wear the trap-pings, And bear not a sol-dier's
mirth; Like warriors to vic - t'ry tread- ing A fire-scorch'd and blood-stain'd

take!" For be- hold how the squadrons mus- ter, And list to the trum- pet's
part; The de -stroy- er is doom'd to per - ish, So prophets and sa - ges
earth; For the war will be stern and dead - ly, And man- y a strong one

blast! 'Tis the war of the Lord Al- might -y, Earth's deadliest and her last.
say; There is safe- ty and hon - or fight- ing, For the Right shall win the day.
fall Ere the ar- mies of darkness per - ish And the sun has risen o'er all.

Be Not Deceived.

D. L. STARR.   J. H. T.

1. As we jour-ney a-long life's rug-ged way, We're sow-ing fruit-ful
2. We sow by the way-side, in the field, On ston-y ground, 'mid
3. Are we sow-ing the seed of tares and sin? A harvest of woe must

seed;.... We sow by night and we sow by day; We
thorus; But the seed we sow will a har-vest yield, Though
come, When the an-gels has-ten to bring it in, And

CHORUS.

sow with word and deed. Oh, be not de-ceived, though
sown in sun or storm.
shout the har-vest home.

con-science sleep! The seed that we sow we'll sure-ly reap; Oh,

be not deceiv'd, tho' conscience sleep, The seed that we sow we'll sure-ly reap!

74

Courage!

C. F. RICHARDSON.

E. A. HOFFMAN.

1. We have chosen to fol - low the cru - ci - fied Lord, Tho' he lead us thro'
2. Our hearts burn within us, for Christ is our guide, His cour-age our
3. Thus bat - tle we ev - er for Christ and the cross; No step we take

dan- gers of fire and of sword; We know not what per - ils a -
cour-age— we fight by his side; Tho' we faint or we fall, we go
backward, no toil we count loss; And brav - est we strug-gle when

wait us be - fore, But the tents we have left we will en - ter no more.
on to the end, The wrong to de - stroy, and the right to de-fend.
dark- est the day, For the hand of our Lead- er still points us the way.

CHORUS.

We will fol - low, we will fol - low the cru - ci - fied Lord; We will

fol-low thro' dan-gers of fire and of sword; What care we for per-ils or suf-fer-ing sore? We will fol-low the Sa-viour for ev-er-more.

Don't Drink To-Night.

MRS. E. C. ELLSWORTH. J. H. TENNEY.

DUET.

1. Don't drink to-night, my boy! Our hearts thine own en-twin-ing, Will
2. Don't drink to-night, my boy! A gen-tle voice is plead-ing, With
3. Don't drink to-night, my boy! An-gel-ic forms at-tend thee To

fill with sad re-pin-ing If Sa-tan thee de-coy.
Je-sus in-ter-ced-ing, Lest sin thy soul de-stroy.
help thee and be-friend thee, And share thy tri-umph joy.

CHORUS.

Don't drink, my boy, to-night! Temp-ta-tion's power de-fy-ing; On Je-sus' strength re-ly-ing, Do thou the right.

76 ## The Temperance Call.

Con spirito.

1. Hear the Temp'rance call, Free - men, one and all! Hear your
2. Leave the shop and farm; Leave your bright hearths warm; To the
3. Hail, our fa - ther - land! Here thy chil - dren stand, All re-

coun - try's earn - est cry; See your na - tive land Lift its
polls! the land to save; Let your lead - ers be True and
solved, u - ni - ted, true, In the Temp'rance cause Ne'er to

beck-'ning hand. "Sons of free - dom, come ye nigh, come ye nigh;
no - ble, free, Fear-less tem - p'rate, good, and brave, good and brave;
faint or pause; This our pur - pose is, and vow; this our vow,

CHORUS.

Chase the mon - ster from our shore; Let his cru - el reign be
Chase the monster from our shore; Let his

o'er Chase the monster from our shore; Let his cru-el reign be o'er."
cru - el reign be o'er from our shore;

DR. H. S. PATERSON.   CHAS. H. GABRIEL.

1. The Lord of Life my death hath died; With him I have been cru ci-fied; Hence-
2. The love of Christ my love hath won; I'm dead and buried with God's Son; Hence-
3. Un-stead-fast once in heart and mind,The sport of ev'ry changeful wind; Hence-

forth in me   sin shall not reign; His grace my tri - umph doth maintain.
forth to him   a - lone   I live; All that he gave to   him   I give.
forth confirm'd in truth and love, On earth I serve my   head   a-bove.

CHORUS.

Christ calls me friend,and tells me still The se -crets of my Fath-er's will; Hence

forth this tie, so strong and sweet,Shall keep me at my Mas-ter's feet, Hence-

forth this tie, so strong and sweet, Shall keep me at my Master's feet.

78 Where are you Going, Young Man?

SOLO AND CHORUS.

FRANK M. DAVIS.

1. Where are you go - ing so fast, young man? Where are you go - ing so
2. Where are you go - ing so fast, young man? Where are you go - ing so
3. A reck-on - ing day is to come, young man, A reck-on- ing day is to

fast...... With a cup in your hand, a flush on your brow? Tho'
fast?.... Oh, the flush of that wine is on - ly a bait! A
come;....There's a life yet to live, a death yet to die, A

pleas-ure and mirth may at-tend you now, It tells of a sor- row to
curse lies beneath that you'll find when too late; A ser-pent sleeps down in the
sad part- ing tear when the hour draws nigh, A jour- ney to take with a

Copyright, 1879, by OLIVER DITSON & Co.

come by and by; It tells of a pang that is sealed with a sigh; It
depths of that cup; A mon-ster is there that will swal-low you up; A
fam - ish - ing heart, A sharp pang to feel from dread death's chilling dart, A

ritard ad lib.

tells of a shame at last, young man, A wither - ing shame that will last.
sor-row you'll find, at last, young man; In wine there is sorrow at last.
curse if you drink that rum, young man, The bit-ter- est curse in that rum.

CHORUS.

Where are you go-ing so fast, young man? Where are you going so fast, With a

cup in your hand, a flush on your brow? O, where are you going, so fast?

There's Danger in the Town.

J. H. T.

1. There, John, hitch Dobbin to the post; come near me, and sit down; Your
2. I've watch'd o'er you from in - fan - cy, till now you are a man, And
3. A mother's eye is searching, John; old age can't dim its sight, When

moth - er wants to talk to you be - fore you drive to town. My
I have al - ways lov'd you as on - ly a mother can; At
watching o'er an on - ly child, to see if he does right; And

hairs are gray; I soon shall be at rest with - in the grave; Not
morn-ing and at evening I have pray'd the God of love To
ver - y late - ly I have seen what has aroused my fears, And

long   will moth-er   pi - lot   you o'er   life's tem- pest-uous wave,   Not
bless   and guide my dar- ling boy to   the bright home a - bove,   To
made   my   pil - low hard at night,and mois-tened it   with tears,   And

rit.

long   will moth-er   pi - lot   you   o'er   life's tem- pest-uous   wave.
bless   and guide my darling   boy   to   the   bright home a - bove.
made   my   pil - low hard at night, and moist-ened   it   with tears.

colla voce.

4 I've seen a light within your eye, upon your cheeks a glow,
That told me you were in the road that leads to shame and woe;
Oh, John, don't turn away your head, and on my counsel frown!
Stay more upon the dear o d farm; there's danger in the town!

5 Your father, John, is growing old; his days are nearly through;
Oh, he has labored very hard to save the farm for you!
But it will go to ruin soon, and povery will frown,
If you keep hitching Dobbin up to drive into the town!

6 Your prospects for the future are very bright, my son;
Not many have your start in life when they are twenty-one;
Your star, that shines so brightly now, in darkness will decline
If you forget your mother's words, and tarry at the wine!

7 Turn back again, my boy, in youth; stay by the dear old farm;
The Lord of hosts will save you with his powerful right arm;
Not long will mother pilot you o'er life's tempestuous wave:
Then light her pathway with your love down to the silent grave!

Gird on the Armor.

H. S. P.

H. S. PERKINS.

With spirit.

1. Gird on the ar- mor, brave soul, to-day; Work for the truth and the right;
2. Storms may as-sail and darkness surround, Thunders of mal- ice a - rise;
2. God's truth will conquer, e'en tho' to-day Er - ror may rule in the land;

Tho' sin and er - ror stand in the way, Darkness will soon take its flight.
Raise high the ban- ner, shout forth the sound, Cloudless will soon be the skies.
Light will pierce darkness, drive gloom away, Firm-ly by truth we will stand.

CHORUS.

Sol- diers of progress, hon- est and true, March to the front 'gainst the wrong;

Those who'd be victors, those who would win, Must be valiant, courageous, and strong.

By permission.

Work, Watch, and Pray.

Mrs. E. C. Ellsworth.

W. Irving Hartshorn.

1. Up, to the work, thyself ad - dressing; Watch, for the foe is sure - ly
2. Work, for the day will soon be wan- ing; Watch, lest the foe should now be
3. Work, for the Lord has so com-mand-ed; Watch, for the foes are strongly

press - ing; Pray for the help we all are need - ing; Work, watch, and
gain - ing; Pray for the prom - ised help is near - ing; Work, watch, and
band - ed; Pray; all is vain with- out a bless - ing; Work, watch, and

CHORUS.

pray, thus la - bor speed- ing.
pray, till Christ's ap- pear- ing.
pray, with care un - ceas- ing.

Work, watch, and pray, thus dai - ly

tax - ing Eye, hand, and heart, nor once re - lax - ing, Till thou the

work shall see complet - ed, Till ev -'ry foe shall be de-feat- ed.

Take Back the Bowl.

WM. COLLINS.   J. H. TENNEY.

Moderato e con passione.

1. Take back the bowl! my lips no more The poisoned draught shall
2. Hardened by sin, and reckless grown, I've quaffed the god - less
3. Take back the bowl! tho' season'd well, There's poi - son in its

drain; The ruth- less de - mon's reign is o'er, And I am free a-
wine, I've bent be - fore the demon's throne, And worshipped at his
breath; It leads to in - fa - my and hell, To sin, and shame, and

By permission.

gain; Free from the stains that soil'd my name, The bonds that bound my
shrine; His toils and wiles were round me cast, To stran - gle,blight, and
death; From out its depths dark sor-rows spring To tor - ture brain and

soul; Free from the guilt,the crime,the shame,That centres in the bowl.
ban; But now his hour at length is past,Once more I breathe,a man.
soul; I scorn the fierce,accursed thing,And spurn the damning bowl.

CHORUS.

Take back the bowl! my lips no more The poisoned draught shall

drain; The ruthless de - mon's reign is o'er, And I am free a- gain!

Not Half has ever been Told.

Rev. J. B. Atchinson.   O. S. Presbrey.

1. I have read of a beau - ti - ful cit - y, Far a -
2. I have read of bright man - sions in hea - ven, Which the
3. I have read of white robes for the right - eous, Of bright
4. I have read of a Christ so for - giv - ing, That vile

way in the kingdom of God; I have read how its walls are of
Saviour has gone to pre - pare, Where the saints who on earth have been
crowns which the glo - ri - fied wear, When our Fa - ther shall bid them, "Come
sin - ners may ask and re - ceive Peace and par - don from ev - 'ry trans -

jas - per, How its streets are all gold - en and broad; In the
faith - ful, Rest for - ev - er with Christ o - ver there; There no
en - ter, And my glo - ry e - ter - nal - ly share;" How the
- gres - sion, If when ask - ing they on - ly be - lieve; I have

By permission.

NOTE. A Skeptic, dying of consumtion, heard his sister sing, " Not Half has ever
been Told," when he cried, "O sister, sing it again! nothing ever so touched my heart,"
So day after day it was sung, to the great comfort of the dying youth. He died singing
" Not half of that city's bright glories to mortals has ever been told."

midst of the streets is life's riv - er,   Clear as   crys - tal, and pure to   be-
sin   ev - er en - ters, nor sor- row;   The in - hab - i- tants nev - er grow
right- eous are ev - er   more bless-ed   As they walk thro' the streets of pure
read how he'll guide and pro-tect us,   If   for safe - ty we en - ter his

hold; But not half of that city's bright glo- ry To mortals has ever been told.
old;   But not half of the joys that await them To mortals has ever been told.
gold; But not half of the wonderful sto - ry To mortals has ever been told.
fold; But not half of his goodness and mercy To mortals has ever been told.

CHORUS.

Not half has ev - er been told,. ...   Not half has ev- er been told,....   Not
been told,   been told,

Repeat the chorus p.

half of that cit-y's bright glo - ry   to mortals has   ev-er been told!

We Pray for You.

REV. E. A. HOFFMAN.   S. H. BLAKESLEE.

1. We have wept o'er the sins that with-held you from Christ, And
2. We have pray'd to the Sa - viour, the cru - ci - fied One, And
3. We will bow at the feet of the Fa - ther a - bove, Who

kept you from tast - ing his love unpriced, And plead with you warm-ly no
laid our pe - ti - tions be- fore the throne. Be-seech- ing the Fa - ther to
loves us with warm-est and tenderest love, And beg him, in ac - cents of

more to de-lay, But haste to the arms of the Saviour away.
turn his face, And bap-tize your soul with his love and grace.
fer - vent prayer, To make you the child of his lov- ing care.

CHORUS.

O - pen your heart, and give him a place, And

he will im-part the joys of his grace, And save you and seal you and cleanse you from sin, And fill you with peace and sweet comfort within.

A Penitent's Plea.

PHŒBE CARY.　　　　　　　　　　　　　　　　　　J. H. T.

1. Like a child that is lost From its home in the night I
2. In the conflicts that pass 'Twixt my soul and my God, I
3. I know the fierce flames Will not cease to up-roll Till thou
4. My thoughts lie with-in me As waste as the sands; O

grope thro' the darkness And cry for the light; Yea, all that is in me Cries
walk as one walketh A fire-path unshod; And in my despair-ing Sit
rain-est the dew Of thy love on my soul; And I know the dumb spir-it Will
make them be mu-si-cal Strings in my hands! My sins, red as scar-let, Wash

out for the day; Come, Je-sus, my Mas-ter, Il-lu-mine my way!
dumb by the way; Come, Je-sus, my Mas-ter, And heal me, I pray!
nev-er de-part' Till thou comest and mak-est Thy house in my heart.
white as the fleece; Come, Je-sus, my Mas-ter, And give me thy peace!

Father, Won't you Try?

A little girl crept upon her father's knee, just after his return from a drunken revel, and plead in tender tones, "Father, won't you stop your drinking? Dearest father, won't you try?"

F. A. HOFFMAN.   MISS SARAH B. HAGAR.

1. Fa - ther, won't you stop your drinking?   It would make our hearts so
2. Fa - ther, don't you pit - y moth - er?   Oft her cheeks are bath'd in
3. And your dar - ling lit - tle Wil - lie   Oft - en calls to us for

glad!   Now our home is   so   un - hap - py,   And we
tears;   Her poor spir - it   has been break- ing,   Lo! these
bread   When the cupboard shelves are emp - ty,   And the

al - ways feel   so sad!   You   would be   so   kind a
ma - ny, man - y years.   Won't   you   be more kind to
hun - gry ones un - fed.   Don't   you love your dar - ling

By permission.

Fa - ther,
moth - er?
Wil- lie?

You could stay each tear and sigh,
She will break her heart and die,
What if he should starve and die!

If you could but cease your drinking; Dearest Father, won't you try?
If you do not stop your drinking; Dearest Father, won't you try?
Won't you stop your drinking, Father? Dearest Father, won't you try?

CHORUS.

Won't you try? won't you try? won't you try? Fa-ther, won't you
won't you try?

try? Won't you stop your drink- ing? Father, won't you try? won't you try?

The Knot of Ribbons Blue.

EBEN E. REXFORD.   R. B. MAHAFFE.

1. I hear a sound of sing-ing Up-on the air to - day, Of
2. The Temp'rance wave sweeps o-ver The land from sea to sea; I
3. Work on, work on, my broth-ers; Be strong to do and dare; Think

glad-ness and thanksgiving, From near and far a - way; I see a band ad-
hear the grand,glad tid-ings Of men from drink set free; And happy wives and
of the shadow'd hearthstones, And weeping women there; Think of the thousands

vanc - ing, Brave,earnest,strong,and true. And on each breast is shin-ing A
moth - ers Rise up, with thanks to God That those they lov'd have follow'd where
sleep - ing To - day in drunkards' graves, And as you work, remember, God

CHORUS.

knot of rib - bons blue. God speed the temp'rance Army; Oh! strong to dare and
onr cru-sa - ders trod.
gives the help that saves.

do Are those who wear its col - ors,— The knot of rib - bons blue.

MRS. E. W. CHAPMAN.   J. H. TENNEY.

1. Haste ye to the fountain's brink, Sparkling in its crys - tal gleam;
2. Gush-ing free - ly from the mount, Flowing from its home a - bove,
3. Sweet-ly glid - ing thro' the vale, Threading soft - ly o'er the lea,

Of its wa - ters free - ly drink; Drink of nature's cool - ing stream,
Em - blem of the liv - ing Fount, Fount of God's un - changing love,
. Spreading lake - lets in the dale, Grand-ly roll-ing to the sea.

CHORUS.

Beau-ti - ful fount, beau-ti - ful fount, Sparkling in the sun - light fair,

Crys - tal wa - ter, pure and cold, We to thee will oft re - pair;

Crys - tal wa - ter, pure and cold, We to thee will oft re - pair.

Cold Water.

MISS H. A. FOSTER.   E. A. H.

1. My pret - ty bird, pray, what do you drink That keeps your voice so
2. Dear bee, so bu - sy, ear - ly, late, And midst un- health- ful
3. Sweet rose, what makes your cheeks so red, Your spir - its al - ways
4. O rose and bee and mer - ry bird, You tell the truth, I'm

clear? You need strong e - lix-irs, I should think, This clime is so se-
dews, Your strength so small, and your work so great, What ton- ic do you
light? Wine gives a glow of good health, 'tis said, If used ex - act - ly
sure; I will remember what I have heard, And, choose a drink that's

vere; The rob - in sang in mer - ry note, "Cold wa - ter for a
use? "The ton - ic found in Flo - ra's cup; I'm al - ways free to
right; The fair rose curled her pret - ty lip, "On - ly pure rains and
pure; The drink for rose and bird and bee, Cold wa - ter, is the

singer's throat; Cold wa - ter, cold wa - ter. Cold wa - ter pure for me."
take a sup; I'm al - ways, yes, al - ways, I'm free to take a sup."
dew I sip; Pure raindrops, pure dew-drops, Pure rain and dew I sip."
drink for me; Cold wa - ter, cold wa - ter, It is the drink for me.

At thy Feet, like Mary.

"She fell down at his feet."—John xi: 32.

E. R. LATTA.   J. H. TENNEY.

1. At thy feet, like Ma - ry   In the days of old,   Fain would bow my
2. At thy feet, like Ma - ry, She of Beth - a - ny,   I would fall, dear
3. At thy feet, like Ma - ry   Of the lov - ing heart, Who, her cares un-

spir - it, And my faith be told;   Go - ing out to meet Him,
Sa - viour, And would worship thee;   She the precious oint - ment
heed - ing, Chose the bet - ter part, I would fall, dear Je - sus,

Tear-ful- ly she cried, " Lord, with thee my brother Would not thus have died! "
In her hand did bear, And his feet anointing, Wiped them with her hair.
As she did of old, To thy voice would listen, And thy face be - hold.

REFRAIN.

At thy feet, like Ma - ry! At thy feet, like Ma - ry,

At thy, feet like Ma - ry In the days of old!

Copyright, 1879, by OLIVER DITSON & Co.

Tell Me of Jesus.

MRS. E. C. ELLSWORTH.   J. H. TENNEY.

1. O tell me of Je-sus! I've heard of his love; I've heard that for
2. O tell me of Je-sus! I've heard that he died; O tell me if
3. O tell me of Je-sus! I've heard that he rose; I've heard that he

sin-ners he came from a-bove; O tell me, tell tru-ly, If
sin-ners the Lord cru-ci-fied! O tell me, tell tru-ly, If
triumphed o'er death and his foes; O tell me, tell tru-ly, If

love for me then Brought Je-sus from glo-ry to dwell a-mong men!
sin nail'd the cross! Yes, tell me if Je-sus for me suf-fered loss.
for us he pleads! Yes, tell me if Je-sus for me in-ter-cedes.

CHORUS.

O yes, we tell tru-ly, yes,
Tru-ly, yes tru-ly we tell thee of Je-sus; We

tru - - ly of Je - - sus; Trust - ing - ly
tell thee so tru - ly, yes, tru - ly of him; Trust-ing- ly, trust-iug - ly,

come, then, for he is thy
come, then, so trust - iug - ly; Trust- iug - ly come, then, for

friend.......... For those who are need - - y, so
he is thy friend. For those so need - y, so need - y and sin - ful, For

need - - y and sin - - ful, He is their
those who are need- y and bur-dened with sin, He is their Saviour, their

Sa - - viour, and loves to the end..........
Sa- viour so pre-cious, Oh, yes! he's their Sa- viour, and loves to the end.

98   Keep a Light in the Window.

"Let your light so shine before men, that they may see your good works, and glorify your Father which is in heaven."—Matt. v. 16.

M. A. MAITLAND.　　　　　　　　　　　　　　　　J. H. TENNEY.

SOLO.

1. Keep a light in the win-dow burn - ing,   Faint tho' its glimm'ring
2. Keep a light in the win-dow burn - ing,   Bril-liant-ly, for a
3. Keep a light in the win-dow burn - ing,   Ye who in God re-

INST.

be;   It may light - en some home-less wan - d'rer
sign,   That up - on you the God of Is - rael
-joice,   And with hope-ful souls are wait - ing The

Tossed up - on life's dark sea;   It may whis - per thoughts of
Mak - eth his face to shine;   Hoping that some long - lost
sound of the Bridegroom's voice   Till the light of his glo - rious

com - fort And hope to the sink - ing heart, Of the
broth - er, Way - laid in the paths of sin, May de-
pres - ence Ex - tin - guish the fee - ble ray, Like the

bea- con that fadeless gleam - eth When the sunbeams of earth de - part.
-scry its wel- come glim - mer And joy - ful - ly en - ter in.
morn-ing star it shall van - ish In the light of the per - fect day.

CHORUS.

Keep a light in the win - dow burn - ing, Faint tho' its glimm'ring

be; It may lighten some homeless wan- d'rer, Toss'd up-on life's dark sea.

Live for Jesus.

"Present yourselves a living sacrifice."—Rom. xii: 1.

E. R. LATTA.　　　　　　　　　　　　　　　　J. H. TENNEY.

1. Live for Je - sus, Live for Je - sus! Give to him thy love;
2. Live for Je - sus, Live for Je - sus! Tho' your work be small;
3. Live for Je - sus, Live for Je - sus! Keep thy earn - est vow;

Lay up ev - er - last - ing treasure Far a - bove. He is wor-thy
He at last will such a ser - vant Faith - ful call. Have you but a
La - bor not for things that per-ish; Serve him now. Live for Je - sus

of thy ser - vice; Work with heart and hand; And in ev - 'ry
sin - gle tal - ent? Use, oh, use it well! At the reap - ing
live for Je - sus! He your Sa - viour is! Strive to be in

CHORUS.

sore tempt - a -tion Thou shalt stand. Live for Je - sus, live for Je - sus
of the har- vest It will tell.
earth and glo - ry Tru - ly his.

While you live! Ev - er-last-ing joy and glo - ry He will give.

Arranged from LYLE.

1. When the voice of du - ty calls, Serve the right! Serve the
2. Tho' the ty - rant boast and frown, Serve the right! Serve the

right! Where the line of la - bor falls, Serve the right! Be the
right! Truth is no - bler than a crown; Serve the right! Ev - 'ry

sta - tion high or low, Let the heart be true and brave; Nev - er
word that hon - or breathes Heav'n in glow - ing light re - cords; Deeds that

fal - ter, nev - er know Trembling fear that mocks the slave; Serve the
ask no lau - rel wreaths Win from heav'n their high re - ward; Serve the

right! Serve the right! Serve the right! Serve the right!
right! Serve the right! Serve the right! Serve the right!

Return, Return.

J. C. J.

HARRY SANDERS.

Written for the BURLL FAMILY.

1. Who are these who roam a - far, When descends the eve-ning star;
2. Hap - py homes all cloth'd in light; Home af - fec - tion, pure and bright;
3. In the dark -ness and the gloom, 'Mid the sha - dows of the tomb,
4. Fa- ther of our sin - ful race In thy grand, a-bounding grace,

Thro' the dark- ness and the night; Whith- er tends their err - ing flight?
Home -ly joys and child - ish glee; These, poor wand'rer, wait for thee!
In the tempter's cru - el pow'r, There they wait the mid-night hour.
Save these souls, to ru - in near, Ere too late, oh, *make* them hear!

Home and pur - est joy they leave, Cheer- ful, trust'ing hearts they grieve,
Life's hard bur-dens well they bear, Who in love the la - bor share,
As the poi - son cup they quaff, As re-sounds the i - diot laugh,
Lead them, by thy pow'rful hand, From that foul and dangerous land,

By permission.

Prayer dis - dain, and love sin - cere, 'Mid the shades they dis- ap-pear!
Trust- ing hop - ing, hand in hand, Journeying to the Heav'nly Land.
Hope re - cedes and dread des- pair Fills the bale-ful sha - dow there.
That, at length, on heav'n's bright shore, They may rest, and roam no more.

REFRAIN.

Ah! re - turn while yet you may re- turn, re - turn! We

From the dark - ness and the gloom............
call, we pray!

Up- ward haste! No more de - lay 'Mid the sha - dows of the tomb!

Oh, Touch not the Wine-Cup!

FRANK M. DAVIS.

1. Oh, touch it not! for deep with-in That ru - by - tint - ed bowl Lie
2. That sparkling glass, if you partake, Will prove your dead-ly foe, And
3. Then pause, ere yet that cup you drain; The hand that lifts it stay; Re-

hid - den fiends of guilt and sin, To grasp the heed-less soul.
may, ere yet its bub - bles break, Have sealed your end - less woe.
solve for - ev - er to ab - stain, And cast the bowl a - way!

CHORUS.

Oh, touch not the wine - cup! The sparkling, tempt - ing
Oh, touch it not! Oh, touch it not!

wine - cup! Oh, touch not the wine - cup! For death, sure death is there!
Oh, touch it not! Oh, touch it not!

The Lord is our Refuge.

D. K. W.

H. S. PERKINS.

1. The Lord is our ref-uge and strength; His prom-is-es nev-er can
2. The won-der-ful pow'r of his love Bends low to hu-man-i-ty's
3. We'll fol-low our heav-en-ly King; His cross is our ban-ner and

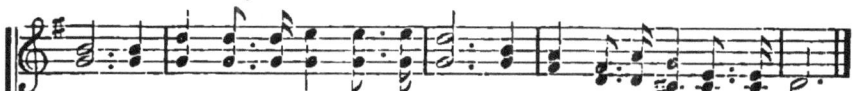

fail; We've learn'd the sweet lesson at length, His grace o-ver sin can pre-vail.
need; Each soul may his faith-ful-ness prove, Each slave by his mercy be freed.
shield; Our all to the con-flict will bring, To conquer or die on the field.

CHORUS.

In the sweet by and by,
In the sweet by and by,
We'll

con-quer the de-mon of rum, bye and bye; In the

sweet bye and bye,
In the sweet bye and bye,
The kingdom of heav'n will come.

By permission.

One by One.

" We spend our years as a tale that is told."—Ps. xv.: 9

MRS. E. W. CHAPMAN.   J. H. TENNEY.

Andante

1. The years, the years are gliding by,   Ev - er and a-
2. The sil - ver thread is in the hair,   Ev - er and a-
3. Per- chance in years thus gliding by,   Ev - er and a-

non; They drop from off the gold-en thread,   One by one; We
non; The eye grows dim, the wrinkles come,   One by one; The
non; We learn the songs that seraph's sing,   One by one; We

can - not gather them a - gain;   They're gone   for   aye.
pleas- ures, once so high - ly prized, Are gone   for   aye.
learn   a   rich and glorious psalm,   To sing   for   aye.

CHORUS.

The gold - en thread of life is break - ing. Soon

One by One. Concluded.

we shall cross the si - lent sea
si - lent sea;
Then on the

shores of life for-ev - er Un - fad - ing joy our eyes may see.

Lead Me Home.

W. C. RICHARDS.

DR. J. A. MUNK, M. D.

Fine.

1. Sa- viour of my trust- ing soul, By thy pas-sion and thy pow'r,
D. C. All its needs thy grace can give, Per - fect - ed in thee to live.
2. In life's des - ert, when I faint, Wea - ry with the load I bear,
D. C. While its burn-ing wastes I tread, Lift thy ban- ner o'er my head.
3. When in sorrow's vale I sigh, Crush'd be-neath a stress of grief,
D. C. Not a tear I shed in vain If thy pit - y soothes my pain.

D.C.

In-to thy di - vine con - trol I would yield it ev - 'ry hour;
O thou strength of ev - 'ry saint! Put thine arms a - round me there.
Solace of my soul, be nigh; On - ly thou canst bring re - lief:

4 When up narrow steeps I pant,
Wounded by the flint and thorn,
Then thy helping hand I want,
Or my heart will sink forlorn;
Leaning on its strength I'll climb
Up to Pisgah's top sublime.

5 Deserts, vales, and hills o'erpast,
At the grave my course will end;
More than ever at the last
I shall need thee, heav'nly Friend,
My last foe to overcome,
And in love to lead me home.

Touch it Not.

J. H. T

1. When you see the rud - dy wine, Touch it not! Touch it not!
2. With tempt-a - tion close at hand, Touch it not! Touch it not!
3. Tho' the rud - dy wine may glow, Touch it not! Touch it not!

Tho' with brightness it may shine, Touch it not! Touch it not!
God will help you to with-stand, Touch it not! Touch it not!
If true hap - pi - ness you'd know, Touch it not! Touch it not!

There is dan - ger in the us - ing, There is safe - ty in re-
Bet - ter far your friendship sev - er Than de- stroy your soul for-
Tho' the ma - gic spell is weav-ing, Still al - lur - ing, still de-

fus - ing; And the lip that once has tast- ed Cannot trust it - self a-gain.
ev - er; And the one that ur - ges is a Fiend, and cannot be a friend.
-ceiv - ing, Be a man, and nev - er, nev- er be entrapp'd in such a snare.

CHORUS.

Of the spark-ling wine be - ware; Touch it not! Touch it

Of your conscience have a care; Touch it not! Touch it not!

Oh, Fling Aloft the Banner.

Mrs. E. C. Ellsworth.   E. H. Bailey.

1. Oh, fling a-loft the ban - ner For Tem-p'rance, for Tem-p'rance! Till
2. Oh, shout a-loud for - ev - er For Tem-p'rance, for Tem-p'rance! Our

Chorus.

D. C. Then fling a-loft the ban - ner For Tem-p'rance, for Temp-p'rance! Till

Fine.

O - ver cot and man - or Shall float the flag that's true;
work shall per - ish nev - er, For Tem-p'rance and for right;

o - ver cot and man - or Shall float the flag that's true.

Oh, yes! our hands are bring-ing, And to the breeze are fling-ing The
Then come, with hearts u-nit - ed, To save the lives now blighted, Till

D.C.

flag whence hope is spring - ing, And lives are made a - new.
ev - 'ry cause is right - ed, And dark - ness turned to light.

110

The Refuge.

REV. EDWIN H. NEVIN, D. D.   W. J. KIRKPATRICK.

1. Help me, help me,   precious Saviour! Help me to   re-nounce my
2. I   have been the slave of pas- sion, Long con - trolled by love of
3. On   thy grace and   lov - ing kindness   I would cast   my wounded
4. Bid   me to   a -   rise in free-dom,   Bid the   fet - ters dis - ap-

sin; Give to me thy conq'ring Spir- it, To re - new   my soul within.
rum. Now, o'erwhelm'd with grief and sorrow, To thy lov - ing heart I come.
soul, Pray - ing thee, the Great Phy-si - cian, Now to   heal and make me whole.
pear, And, with thy strong arm beneath me   My re- demp- tion will be near.

CHORUS.

Help me, help me, precious Sa - viour! Hear my earn - est, pleading

cry; I would trust in   thee for-ev - er, On thy promised aid re - ly.

INDEX.

www.ingramcontent.com/pod-product-compliance
Lightning Source LLC
Chambersburg PA
CBHW031441280326
41927CB00038B/1476